TALKING ABOUT

*Six interchurch discussion booklets based o
conversations worldwide*

BOOKLET FOUR

Ministry

G. R. Evans

THE CANTERBURY PRESS NORWICH

The Canterbury Press Norwich, St Mary's Works,
St Mary's Plain, Norwich, Norfolk NR3 3BH

The Canterbury Press Norwich is a publishing imprint
of Hymns Ancient & Modern Limited

ISBN 0 907547 60 5

First published 1986

© G. R. Evans

All rights reserved. No part of this publication which is copyright may be reproduced, stored in a retrieval system, or transmitted, in any form or by any means, electronic, mechanical, photocopying, recording, or otherwise, without the prior permission of The Canterbury Press Norwich or the appropriate copyright owner.

Printed in Great Britain at the
University Press, Cambridge

A booklist

Christian communities have lately been talking to one another on several fronts. You can find an account of the way these dialogues began and a summary of what they have achieved so far in *Anglicans in Dialogue*, Church of England Board for Mission and Unity, 1984, and of others in *Growth and Unity*, (see below).

Abbreviations used in these booklets

BEM	*Baptism, Eucharist and Ministry*. Faith and Order Paper 111. World Council of Churches, 1982.
ARCIC	*The Final Report of the Anglican–Roman Catholic International Commission*. SPCK/CTS, 1982
AL	*Anglican–Lutheran Dialogue: the Report of the European Commission*. SPCK, 1983.
AR	*God's Reign and Our Unity: the Report of the Anglican–Reformed International Commission*. SPCK/St Andrew Press, 1984.
AO	*Anglican–Orthodox Dialogue: the Dublin Agreed Statement, 1984*. SPCK, 1984.
Resp.	*Towards a Church of England Response to BEM and ARCIC*. CIO, 1985.

You can buy a collection of *Reports and Agreed Statements of Ecumenical Conversations on a World Level*, ed.

H. Meyer and L. Vischer (World Council of Churches, Geneva, 1984), called *Growth in Unity*.

The Bookshop, Church House, Dean's Yard, Westminster, London SW1P 3NZ, can supply all these by post, or your local bookshop can get them for you if you want to read the Reports for yourself.

Some books on Ministry:

Buchanan, C. (ed.). *Whose Hand on the Tiller?* Grove Pastoral Studies, no. 16.
Schillebeeckx, E. *The Church with a Human Face*. SCM, 1985.
Simpson, R. *How We Grew a Local Ecumenical Project*. Grove Pastoral Studies, no. 17.
Tiller, J. *A Strategy for the Church's Ministry (The Tiller Report)*. CIO, 1983.

4. Ministry

The Ministry of all faithful people.

There has always been a ministry of the whole Church in which all Christians share.

In a broken world God calls the whole of humanity to become God's people... The Holy Spirit unites in a single body those who follow Jesus Christ and sends them as witnesses into the world.

BEM, Ministry, 1

The company gathered behind closed doors on that first Easter evening was the Church in embryo. It is to the whole Church that the commission is given... This ministry is exercised by and through the entire membership of the Church in the course of their daily work in the world.

AR, 74

Together with other Churches, Anglicans and Lutherans are rediscovering the importance of the ministry of the whole People of God, the general priesthood of all baptised believers.

AL, 34

What gifts of ministry do you see in yourself and your friends?

How could they best be used in the local ministry of your parish?

Dusting the pews

For Discussion:

Some church members, including clergy, need specific inner healing before they can begin to believe that they are capable of ministry. Many are so hurt by rejection, failure, and disapproval, their self-image is so damaged, and their sense of self-worth so low, that they need the deep affirmation of God's Spirit that they are children of God and fellow-heirs with Christ (Rom. 8. 17)... We need to foster that kind of congregational life which encourages people to believe in themselves and take the necessary risks involved in discovering the gifts they have. Probably nothing causes gifts to emerge as much as encouragement.

Whose Hand on the Tiller? pp. 15–16

Arranging the flowers is more fun than dusting the pews

What helps and what hinders us in sharing our individual gifts of ministry?

Does competitiveness get in the way of trust and freedom?
(How do you decide who is to do a job everyone would like? Arranging the flowers is more fun than dusting the pews.)

Do cliques form because people want to stick with the group in which they have grown in trust and openness?

Is divisiveness a problem when one or more small groups press for movement and action?

Have any of these disorders of harmony which prevent our working together peacefully and constructively arisen in your own congregation? What have you learned about how best to handle them?

Does experience suggest that the Church in each local place benefits from having someone to act as leader and 'shepherd'?

Would you like to see each congregation choose its own leader?

What authority would such a leader have?

Could such a leader act as a link between the universal Church and the local congregation?

It is clear from the Bible that the leaders of the early Christian community were chosen and sent primarily by God himself, even if through the community.

Calling

Read Ephesians 4. 1–16, in which St Paul describes how Christians are all called 'to keep the unity of the Spirit in the bond of peace', but certain individuals are called to specific ministry, as pastors, teachers, preachers and so on.

Sending

In Acts 13. 1–4 we read how the Holy Spirit sent Barnabas and Saul, choosing them specially for the work they were to do. This 'sending' echoes Jesus' sending out of his disciples to preach the Gospel and heal the sick. And that sending was itself a result of the Father's sending the Son into the world to preach peace and reconciliation and to bring healing to his people.

The Church as a whole, and all ministry with and on behalf of the Church, have one source in the action of the Father in

sending the Son into the world anointed by the Spirit to announce and embody God's blessed reign over all humankind and all creation. For the fulfilment of this mission Jesus called others to follow him and – in particular – appointed twelve 'to be with him and that he might send them out to preach and to have authority to cast out demons' (Mark 3. 14 ff.)

After his final victory over the powers of evil, Jesus returned to assure these disciples that he was still with them, giving them the gift of his peace, sending them into the world to continue his mission, giving them his Spirit, and entrusting to them the ministry of release from sin and reconciliation with the Father (John 20. 19–23).

AR, 73

This ministry is a special gift of God, related to the ministry of all faithful people, but distinct from it, too. There is something extra about it:

Have you been in a group of people brought to life and filled with purpose by a leader with gifts to inspire and motivate them?

Have you ever found the example or the words of a dedicated person having a deep influence on you?

Has someone ever been of special help to you by caring about your difficulties and taking time to listen or doing something practical?

Has anyone ever helped you to come closer to God?

How is the ministry of all faithful people related to the ordained ministry?

Although Christ is the model of all ministry, there is a rich diversity of ministry among his people, all springing from him as its source, and all inspired by him. In all its different ways this ministry builds up the Church as a community of reconciliation.

The variety includes the common priesthood of the faithful and the ordained ministry in an ordered relationship to one another, so that each in its own proper way shares the one priesthood of Christ.

When we speak of the 'apostolic Church' in the Creeds we are saying that the Church carries on the work the apostles were sent by Christ to do in the world. That involves the whole Church. But certain individuals have a particular responsibility, as the apostles themselves did. They are given a distinct gift of ministry, so that they can serve the Church in specific ways. They have the same status as all faithful people, but they have a particular function.

> Their ministerial commission is to be shepherds of the flock
> to care for the preaching of the word and the sacraments and
> to perform particular actions in the name of Christ

for the service of his people. They 'focus' the work of the Church.

Ministry is the Gift of God to the Church

All a minister's qualifications come from God as a gift (2 Corinthians 3. 5–6). He is equipped by the Holy Spirit to fulfil his priestly task in everyday life as well as within the Christian community (AL, 34).

He responds by offering himself, his life and commitment in bearing witness to Christ and in serving others (AL, 34).

Ministry is also a gift to the Church as a whole, made through its individual ordained ministers.

Ministry is always a function within the Church. It has no existence apart from the Church because it exists to serve the people who make up the Church. If it is to be recognised the commission must be given through those who have been commissioned, like links in a historic chain.

That means that no one can legitimately set himself up as the pastor of a congregation solely because he believes that the Holy Spirit has called him to do so. He must also be recognised and called through and by the Church, and given Christ's authority through the Church and in the Church (Ephesians 4. 11–12).

So the ordained ministry is doubly 'sent'. Such ministers receive the gift of the Spirit and are appointed by the Church for service by ordination through the invocation of the Spirit and the laying on of hands (BEM, Ministry, 7).

This appointment by the Church is from Christ. The power of ordination which the Church exercises is not its own but his.

At ordination, the minister is called and sent not only by God himself, but also by God's people, joining in an action of the whole apostolic community of believers.

What does the ordained minister do?

The ordained minister does what all Christians do in their ministry, in a concentrated way. But he also acts on behalf of the whole community in a ministry *to* the Church.

- The ordained minister is a steward of the gifts of the Holy Spirit.

- He can provide for his people only what belongs to Christ.

- It is his special responsibility,
  publicly and continually,

to strengthen and build up
the royal and prophetic priesthood of the faithful.

- He stands in the world but at the same time apart from it
as an example of holiness and compassion,
representing Christ,
proclaiming his message of reconciliation as an ambassador from him,
a channel to bring God to humanity and humanity to God,
by which the holy can communicate with the unholy.

- He does this by preaching the Word of God,
by celebrating the sacraments,
by prayers of intercession,
by pastoral guidance of the community,
by bearing humanity's miseries,
by speaking up for the cause of justice and peace.

- He seeks in all these ways and by all these means to bring about the reconcilation between man and God which Christ made possible.

Two actions above all are special actions of the ordained minister:

(1) Presiding at the sacrament of our redemption,

Holy Communion. (There is more about that in the pamphlet on the Eucharist.)

(2) Declaring God's forgiveness.

Every Christian can do that by putting his trust in the forgiveness which is extended to humanity through the work of Christ. But what about the person who has done something he knows to be seriously wrong and who is in great distress of conscience about it? He needs someone who has the training to meet his particular need, and who can assure him that he is forgiven, by the authority Christ has given him as an ordained minister to forgive sins (John 20. 23).

All agree that the essential elements in the service or rite of ordination are prayer for the gift of the Spirit for the specific task and commission, together with the laying on of hands. The New Testament speaks of the 'gift' bestowed by the laying on of hands (1 Timothy 4. 14; 2 Timothy 1. 6). So there is an inward and invisible gift accompanying and conveyed through the outward action of the Church. Moreover, the Church understands this commission to be more than an *ad hoc* or temporary commission to last for a year or a week, but rather to be a calling to life-long dedication.

The content of the commission also needs to be defined.

(*a*) First and foremost, the priest (or bishop) is given

a commission to preach the gospel. Here the person ordained is the focus or centre of the commission given to the whole people of God. By ordination it becomes his specific task to proclaim the gospel to the particular place where he is sent.

(*b*) Although the bishop and priest are publicly called to a wide task of proclaiming the gospel and of caring for the people entrusted to them, there are also very specific tasks assigned to them. The most prominent of these is that of presiding at the celebration of the Lord's Supper, the great 'thanksgiving' (or eucharist), the memorial of Christ's sacrifice and receiving of his presence and very self. Because 'the eucharist is a making present of the once-for-all sacrifice of Christ' (AR 68), the action of the president and of the whole congregation is pervaded by sacrificial language. That is, the bread is broken and the wine poured out in representation of the redeeming death of Christ, and by receiving the sacred elements the communicants participate in that sacrifice (1 Corinthians 10, 16). So, while there is a unique sense in which Christ is high priest of the whole body of the Church, there is a priestliness both in the entire Church and also in the president of the eucharistic celebration.

By ordination the bishop or priest is commissioned and empowered to do what he does.

As a sign that he does not act on his own private authority, he may be given a Bible, or the sacred vessels, plate and cup (called paten and chalice) – symbols of what he is empowered and sent to do.

(*c*) The gospel is both about the forgiveness of sins and about the renewal or regeneration of the heart with the new life of the Spirit; and these themes are very prominent in the service of baptism.

But baptised Christians fall into sins – some little faults, daily healed as we say the Lord's Prayer with its petition for forgiveness, but in other cases the sins can be very serious. One of the tasks to which a priest is called and commissioned is not only to declare the fact of God's forgiving mercy to the penitent but also to deal pastorally with individuals. Where these individuals give good reason to judge that they are or wish to be truly penitent, confessing their faults and determined to make amends, then the priest is empowered to pronounce absolution, in the name of Christ and his Church.

To think about

Does it make any difference whether the minister says 'I declare that in the sight of God your sins are forgiven' or speaks as the channel of that forgiveness: 'Almighty God, who forgives all who truly repent, have mercy upon you, pardon and deliver you from all your sins'?

Bishops, Priests and Deacons

In the Roman Catholic, Orthodox, Anglican, Lutheran and some other communions a group of ordained ministers exercise a higher responsibility still, as bishops.

During the first Christian centuries a pattern of threefold ministry emerged.

In the beginning these three ministries were the ministries of the local church. The bishop was the shepherd and leader of the local community, he presided over the celebration of the Eucharist. He was surrounded by a college of presbyters who with him had the responsibility of teaching, preaching and leadership. He was assisted by deacons who gave special attention to the diaconal witness of the community [that is, to the pastoral care of the people].

AR, 93

This 'college' or group of presbyters (priests) working with the bishop kept a good balance between the aspects which must be present in all ministry: its personal character and its 'collegial' character. That is, a specific person provides 'a focus for the unity and witness of the community', and at the same time there is a sharing of ministerial responsibility within a fellowship of colleagues (AR, 92).

With the growth of the Church and the consequent pressure of numbers, this pattern changed until it looked more like the structure we know today.

The bishop became the leader of several congregations while the presbyters became the shepherds of these congregations. In this way, and no doubt for good reasons, the bishop's office gradually became a regional one.

AR, 93

Today, priests usually serve a local church while bishops look after a large number of churches in a diocese.

Presbyters [priests] serve as pastoral ministers of Word and sacraments in a local eucharistics community. They are preachers and teachers of the faith, exercise pastoral care and bear responsibility for the discipline of the congregation to the end that the world may believe and that the entire membership of the church may be renewed, strengthened and equipped in ministry.

BEM, Ministry, 30

That is not to say that the threefold ministry must always be the pattern of Christian ministry everywhere. In fact, after the sixteenth century it ceased to be universal. But there is no doubt that 'it developed from the New Testament period' and is therefore a very early pattern in the Church.

The ARCIC commission suggests that it came into being 'under the guidance of the Holy Spirit and is of God', language which directly echoes one of the Church of England's greatest thinkers, Richard Hooker. The BEM text also suggests that such a pattern 'may serve today as an expression of the unity we seek and also as a means for achieving it' (BEM, Ministry 22).

What advantages and disadvantages can you see in the threefold ministry as you have experienced it?

'Shepherds of the flock'

What are the special responsibilities of the bishop?

(1) *As a 'Shepherd'*

(*a*) He must lead and guide the priests and deacons under his care.

'Fishers of men'

(*b*) He must ordain new priests and deacons from among the people, taking care to see that they are suitable and properly trained and believe themselves to be called to ordination by the Holy Spirit.

(*c*) He must get to know his people personally and not leave it to his priests and deacons to work among them.

(*d*) He must bring the Church's discipline to bear when it is necessary.

(2) *As a 'Bridge'*

The bishop must be a connecting link which unites his own people with the rest of the Christian community. He carries on the work of the Apostles which has continued in every age and is thus an important means of making his people one with Christians of the past and of the future. In the same way he acts as a bridge between his own flock and those of other bishops.

(3) *As a Guardian and Teacher of the Faith*

(*a*) He must be a guardian of the faith and of the tradition by which the Church has transmitted it generation by generation.

(*b*) He must himself teach and watch over the Christian teaching and theological discussion which goes on in his diocese.

This is all summed up in the Lima Report in terms which underline the fact that the bishop carries out all these tasks within the ministry of the whole church. He is like a parent to growing children not the master of servants, and his children become able to join in for themselves as they 'grow up'.

What are Deacons?

Deacons, though not...empowered to preside at the eucharist and to pronounce absolution...are associated with bishops and presbyters in the ministry of word and sacrament, and to assist in oversight.
ARCIC, Ministry, 9

In principle it can be a lifelong vocation to serve as a deacon. It has become normal that deacons are ordained in due course to the priesthood, and then they are able to carry out the two priestly actions of presiding at the Eucharist and forgiving sins.

So, in many communions, the diaconate has become a stepping-stone to the priesthood, and has largely lost its distinctive character, so that the threefold ministry has almost become a twofold ministry (bishop–priest, minister–elder) in a number of Churches (AR, 91).

Practical care

But in the early Church deacons were appointed for a particular task which was a ministry in its own right. In Acts 6. 1–6 you can read how seven men, full of the Holy Spirit, were chosen to take care of the practical affairs of the community. That left the apostles free to preach and teach.

Is this a separation of responsibilities which makes sense today? Would it be useful to have deacons who concentrated on the traditional tasks which were done by deacons in the first Christian communities, and did not go on to be priests?

Deacons represent to the Church its calling as servant in the world. By struggling in Christ's name with the myriad needs of societies and persons, deacons exemplify the interdependence of worship and service in the Church's life. They exercise responsibility in the worship of the congregation... They help in the teaching of the congregation. They exercise a ministry of love within the community. They fulfil certain administrative tasks and may be elected to responsibilities for governance.
BEM, Ministry, 31

Deacons who are ordained priest or bishop do not of course cease to be deacons. The serving ministry is a mark of all three orders.

Some terms which cause difficulty

(1) Priesthood

'The priesthood of Christ is unique' (ARCIC, Ministry, Elucidation, 2; BEM, Ministry, 17).

Yet many churches uses the word 'priest' for certain ordained ministers. How can a name which is special to

Christ be applied to a human being even if acting as his representative?

In the celebration of the Eucharist as a memorial of Christ's sacrifice, Christians saw Christ's priesthood reflected in the minister who presided (Resp. 203). It is by reflection or as an analogy, then, that a human minister is called a priest. He does as Christ's minister acts of service to the community which are the work of Christ himself done through him, 'strengthening and building up the faithful through word and sacrament, through prayers of intercession, through pastoral guidance of the community' (BEM, Ministry, 17).

Some churches still prefer to avoid the use of the word 'priest' and use 'minister', 'pastor', or some other alternative.

What arguments for and against using the word 'priest' can you see? Do we attribute to a human being more than he can carry when we call him a priest? Do we leave out something central to ordained ministry if we do not call him a priest?

(2) *'Apostolic'*

In Acts 2. 42 you can read Luke's account of the life of the early Church:

> hearing the apostles' teaching

> breaking bread together as Jesus had told them to do
>
> praying together
>
> enjoying one another's fellowship in the community (*koinonia*) (Resp. 198).

Read Mark 10. 43–5; Acts 20. 28; 1 Timothy 4. 12–16; 1 Peter 5. 1–4

All Christian ministry is derived from Christ's own ministry through:

> the relationship the first apostles had with Christ while he lived on earth
>
> the commission he gave them, to the Church and to the world
>
> (ARCIC, Ministry, 4)

The early Christian community Luke describes was doing two things:

> carrying out the mission of preaching the Gospel Jesus entrusted to his disciples
>
> living in *koinonia*, in fellowship with one another and with him.

These two things are inseparable in the life of the

Church. Acts 1. 28 emphasises how important the apostles thought it that they should witness to the resurrection of Jesus. It was in this way that their personal relationship with Christ opened the way after his death and resurrection for the spread of the Church in the world.

The essential elements in apostolic ministry are, then,

(i) the fellowship, the relationship with Christ, which makes the ministry Jesus committed to the apostles the same ministry we share today,

(ii) and the unbroken succession of 'sending' which has gone on from the beginning. (The word 'apostolic' means 'to do with mission'.)

Is it important that this succession should involve a physical and historical continuity of laying on of hands from the beginning until now? What other kinds of continuity are involved? Can we see a continuity of commitment and purpose?

For discussion

(1) *The reconciliation of ministries*

If Christians are to unite in the celebration of the Eucharist, everyone present must recognise that the minister who presides has authority to do so. One of the results of division in the Church has always been a refusal to accept the validity of one another's ordained ministries. This refusal is the greatest practical bar to shared communion.

But it is a symptom of division, not a cause. If Christians are reconciled with one another they will no longer find it much of a problem to recognise one another's ministries.

Have ministers of other denominations been invited to preach in your Church?

In what other ways could you learn about the pattern of ministry in other denominations?

(2) *The ordination of women*

There is in Christ no male or female (Galatians 3. 28)... The Church must discover the ministry which can be provided by women as well as that which can be provided by men.
BEM, Ministry, 18

The Lima text says nothing about the detailed working out of this process of 'discovery'. But it is going on very actively at present in many Christian communions. There is a good deal of disagreement about it, and the Reports are all cautious.

The question at issue is this:

In Western society women have successfully struggled for more or less equal rights with men, and have access to careers (and salaries) comparable with those of their male colleagues. Some women find their fulfilment as human beings in running a home and bringing up children; others want to work in areas traditionally the province of men, and it is now possible for them to do so, in most cases. But they cannot yet become priests in the Roman Catholic, Orthodox or Anglican Churches (except in the Anglican communion in the U.S.A. and some other parts of the world). It can seem that the Church is backward in recognising their equality with men; it is tempting for women to turn away in inward alienation from the Christian tradition, and from the Church whose backbone they have been for the greater part of its history.

On the other hand, there is little doubt that both Scripture and long tradition assume that the representative priestly task is one that should be given to men.

The problem is to determine whether

(1) this is a reflection of an obsolete social order, or

(2) an expression of profound psychological insight about the inherent character of the Church's sacred tradition.

Christian communions which set great value on continuity and tradition (such as Roman Catholics and Orthodox and a body of Anglicans) tend to adopt the second view.

Protestant bodies other than strongly biblicist conservatives (who believe what St Paul says about women's place in the Church is a permanent guide-line for all time) have tended to take the first view.

The Vatican issued a negative statement (*Inter insigniores*) on 15 October 1976 to discourage Roman Catholics from supporting this idea, but among individual Roman Catholics, 'high' Anglicans and even Orthodox there are those who would agree with the first view and argue that there is now no reason why women should not be ordained priest.

One of the questions now facing the Church of England is whether it can make a decision about this on its own, since if it decides to admit women to the priesthood it will widen the gulf separating it from Roman Catholic and Orthodox, and therefore from the pre-Reformation tradition which the Church of England also represents.

On the other hand, the representativeness of the priesthood is much diminished if a substantial number of Christian women have ceased to feel that in an exclusively male priesthood they are in fact represented.

At the Church of England's General Synod in November 1984 all three Houses voted to explore the practical steps to be taken towards the ordination of women to the priesthood. In July 1985 it was agreed that women could and should be ordained as deacons.

Where do you think we should go from here?